Pamphlet Series No. 51

Debt Relief for Low-Income Countries

The Enhanced HIPC Initiative

David Andrews, Anthony R. Boote,
Syed S. Rizavi, and Sukhwinder Singh

INTERNATIONAL MONETARY FUND
Washington, D.C.
1999

Revised November 1999

ISSN 0538-8759
ISBN 1-55775-880-8

Production: IMF Graphics Section
Cover design: Luisa Menjivar-Macdonald
Figures: In-Ok Yoon
Typesetting: Alicia Etchebarne-Bourdin

Contents

The following symbols have been used throughout this pamphlet:

. . . to indicate that data are not available;

— to indicate that the figure is zero or less than half the final digit shown, or that the item does not exist;

– between years or months (e.g., 1996–97 or January–June) to indicate the years or months covered, including the beginning and ending years or months;

/ between years (e.g., 1996/97) to indicate a crop or fiscal (financial) year.

"Billion" means a thousand million.

Minor discrepancies between constituent figures and totals are due to rounding.

The term "country," as used in this pamphlet, does not in all cases refer to a territorial entity that is a state as understood by international law and practice; the term also covers some territorial entities that are not states, but for which statistical data are maintained and provided internationally on a separate and independent basis.

Preface

Since the debt crisis of the 1980s the international financial community has been providing help to debtor countries in reducing their external debt burdens in order to foster growth, reduce poverty, and attain external viability. This assistance has taken the form of the provision of concessional financing from international financial institutions, debt relief from official creditors mainly in the context of Paris Club reschedulings, and, in some cases, through bilateral action by the creditors. These measures have resulted in considerable success in alleviating the external debt burdens of many middle-income countries. Many poor countries, especially those in sub-Saharan Africa, however, continue to suffer from unacceptable levels of poverty and heavy external debt burdens owing to a combination of factors, including imprudent external debt-management policies, lack of perseverance in structural adjustment and economic reform, deterioration in their terms of trade, and poor governance.

To address the problems of these countries, the World Bank and the IMF in September 1996 jointly launched the Initiative for the Heavily Indebted Poor Countries (HIPCs) with the aim of reducing the external debt burdens of all the eligible HIPCs to a "sustainable" level in a reasonably short period of time. This pamphlet describes the rationale for and the main features of the Initiative as it was originally conceived in 1996 and its implementation through the fall of 1999. It then goes on to describe the review process launched in early 1999, which culminated in the approval of an enhanced HIPC Initiative in late 1999 that is aimed at providing deeper and more rapid debt relief to a larger number of countries. The enhanced HIPC Initiative also seeks to ensure that debt relief is integrated into a comprehensive poverty reduction strategy that is developed with broad-based participation and tailored to the country's circumstances.

The authors wish to acknowledge with thanks the helpful comments of Russell Kincaid and Doris Ross of the Policy Development and Review Department. Thanks are also due to Jeff Hayden of the External Relations Department for editorial assistance, and to Sulochana Kamaldinni and Seetha Milton for secretarial support.

The views and opinions expressed in the pamphlet are those of the authors and do not necessarily reflect the views of the IMF or of its Executive Directors.

The Enhanced Initiative for Heavily Indebted Poor Countries (HIPCs)

Countries affected by the debt crisis of the 1980s received concerted support from the international financial community in the form of Paris Club flow reschedulings (rescheduling of debt service falling due), stock-of-debt operations (reduction in the stock of outstanding debt) under the Brady plan, and adjustment programs supported by the multilateral financial institutions. These measures proved effective in significantly improving the debt situation of many middle-income countries. A number of poor countries, especially those in sub-Saharan Africa, however, continued to face difficulties in meeting their external debt-servicing obligations because of a confluence of factors. These included the accumulation—through, among other things, provision by creditors of official export credits and poor external debt-management strategies in the debtor countries—of significant nonconcessional debt, a deterioration in debtors' terms of trade, vagaries of weather, protracted civil wars, weak economic policies, and weaknesses in governance.[1]

The international community increasingly recognized that the unsustainable external debt situation of heavily indebted poor countries was becoming one of the sources of slow economic growth, persistent poverty, and weak social policies in these countries.[2] To address this situation, the

---

[1]See Brooks and others, "External Debt Histories of Ten Low-Income Developing Countries: Lessons from Their Experience," IMF Working Paper No. 98/72, May 1998.

[2]A group of 41 developing countries were classified as being heavily indebted poor countries. This group included, for analytical purposes, 32 countries with a 1993 GNP per capita of $695 or less and a 1993 present value of debt to exports higher than 220 percent, or present value of debt to GNP higher than 80 percent. Also included were nine countries that received, or were eligible for, concessional rescheduling from Paris Club official creditors. However, any other country meeting the requirements of the Initiative could also be considered for HIPC Initiative assistance.

The group of 41 countries consisted of Angola, Benin, Bolivia, Burkina Faso, Burundi, Cameroon, Central African Republic, Chad, Congo, Côte d'Ivoire, Democratic Republic of the Congo, Equatorial Guinea, Ethiopia, Ghana, Guinea, Guinea-Bissau, Guyana, Honduras, Kenya, Lao PDR, Liberia, Madagascar, Mali, Mauritania, Mozambique, Myanmar, Nicaragua, Niger, Nigeria, Rwanda, São Tomé and Principe, Senegal, Sierra Leone, Somalia, Sudan, Tanzania, Togo, Uganda, Vietnam, Yemen, and Zambia. Malawi was subsequently added to the group.

IMF and the World Bank in September 1996 jointly adopted the HIPC Initiative to reduce the debt burdens of eligible HIPCs to sustainable levels, provided they adopt and carry out strong programs of macroeconomic adjustment and structural reforms.

This pamphlet explains the rationale for, and main features of, the Initiative as originally conceived in 1996 and the implementation of the Initiative through late 1999, and then describes the review process launched in early 1999, which culminated in the approval of a strengthened HIPC Initiative designed to deliver deeper debt relief more rapidly to a wider range of countries. The pamphlet emphasizes the aggregate aspects of the HIPC Initiative. More detailed information on the external debt situations and economic and social polices of individual countries that have entered into the Initiative is available in country-specific HIPC documents, which are posted on the IMF's website (http://www.imf.org).

The Initial Framework

The Initiative is intended to deal comprehensively with the overall external debt burden of eligible countries, reducing it to a sustainable level within a reasonable period of time. A country can be considered to achieve external debt sustainability if it is expected to be able to meet its current and future external debt-service obligations in full, without recourse to debt relief, rescheduling of debts, or the accumulation of arrears, and without compromising growth.

Key Features

The HIPC Initiative is based on the following principles:

- The Initiative targets overall debt sustainability on a case-by-case basis, thus providing a permanent exit from the rescheduling process.
- Creditors envisage providing debt relief only after the debtor country has demonstrated the capacity to use prudently whatever debt relief is granted.
- Additional debt relief is granted on top of existing (traditional) debt-relief mechanisms.[3]
- Debt-relief measures under the Initiative are coordinated among all creditors involved, with broad and equitable participation.
- Steps taken by multilaterals are in line with their status as preferred creditors and will preserve their financial integrity.
- New financing for the HIPCs is on appropriately concessional terms.

[3]Traditional debt-relief mechanisms include the adoption of stabilization and economic reform programs supported by concessional loans from the IMF and the World Bank; in support of these adjustment programs, flow-rescheduling agreements with Paris Club creditors on concessional terms (such as a 67 percent net present value reduction under Naples terms) followed by a stock-of-debt operation after three years of good track records under both the IMF arrangements and rescheduling agreements; agreement by the debtor country to seek at least comparable terms on debt owed to non-Paris Club bilateral and commercial creditors facilitated by IDA debt-reduction operations on commercial debt; bilateral forgiveness of official development assistance debt by many creditors; and new financing on appropriately concessional terms. See footnote 14 for estimates of debt relief under the traditional mechanisms.

Eligibility Under the Initiative

The criteria for eligibility under the Initiative reflect both the principles underlying the Initiative and a broad-based consensus of member governments that the poorest countries should have the highest priority in concessional debt relief. Specifically, eligibility for receiving exceptional assistance is limited to countries eligible for International Development Association (IDA) loans and for the Enhanced Structural Adjustment Facility (ESAF) that have established strong track records of performance under programs supported by the IMF and the World Bank and that are not expected to achieve a sustainable external debt situation even after the full use of traditional debt-relief mechanisms.

The key indicator of external debt sustainability used in the Initiative is the ratio of the net present value (NPV) of debt to exports.[4] Under the initial framework of the Initiative applied through the fall of 1999, assistance was only provided where necessary to bring the NPV of debt—after the full use of traditional mechanisms—to a range of 200 to 250 percent of exports. The target NPV of debt-to-export ratio within this range for a qualifying country was determined using country-specific "vulnerability factors"; these include the concentration and variability of export earnings, the fiscal burden of external debt service, external debt in relation to GDP, the resource gap, the level of international reserves, and the burden of private sector debt.

In addition, countries with very open economies (defined as having an export-to-GDP ratio of at least 40 percent) and making strong efforts to generate revenue (indicated by fiscal revenues of at least 20 percent of GDP) could also be considered eligible for assistance under the Initiative if the NPV of their debt exceeded 280 percent of government revenues.

[4]The face value of the external debt stock is not a good measure of a country's debt burden if a significant part of the external debt is contracted on concessional terms with an interest rate below the prevailing market rate. The NPV of debt is a measure that takes into account the degree of concessionality. It is defined as the sum of all future debt-service obligations (interest and principal) on existing debt, discounted at the market interest rate. Whenever the interest rate charged for a loan is lower than the market interest rate, the resulting NPV of debt is smaller than its face value, with the difference reflecting the grant element. This measure can also provide an assessment of the total debt burden. In contrast, the debt-service ratio in any one year captures only the immediate cash flow impact of external debt and is strongly influenced by the maturity structure of the underlying debts.

Implementation of the Initiative

To qualify for assistance under the Initiative, an eligible country enters into a macroeconomic reform and structural adjustment program supported by the IMF and the World Bank, with concessional financing. The requirement of establishing a track record is intended to ensure that countries are in a position to use the additional resources effectively. In support of their adjustment programs, the debtor country also receives flow-reschedulings from Paris Club official creditors on Naples terms (67 percent NPV reduction) and seeks at least comparable treatment from non-Paris Club official bilateral and commercial creditors on debt owed to them. After successfully establishing a track record for three years (first stage) under these adjustment programs and rescheduling agreements with the Paris Club, a country reaches its *decision point* (see Figure 1). At the decision point, the Executive Boards of the IMF and World Bank determine the country's eligibility for assistance under the Initiative on the basis of the results of a comprehensive (loan-by-loan) debt sustainability analysis agreed jointly by IMF and World Bank staff and the country authorities. The results of the debt sustainability analysis allow the Boards to assess whether the full application of traditional debt-relief mechanisms (Paris Club stock-of-debt operation on Naples terms involving a 67 percent NPV reduction with at least comparable action from non-Paris Club official bilateral and commercial creditors) would be sufficient for the country to reach the targeted levels of debt indicators, or whether assistance would be required under the Initiative.

Where a country is deemed eligible for assistance under the Initiative, the assistance is delivered at the *completion point*. During the period between the decision point and the completion point (the second or interim stage), the country continues implementing macroeconomic reform and structural adjustment polices supported by concessional lending from the IMF and World Bank. At the same time, Paris Club creditors provide flow reschedulings on Lyon terms (involving up to 80 percent NPV reduction) as needed on a case-by-case basis and commit to providing at the completion point a stock-of-debt operation on Lyon terms, provided the program supported by the IMF and the World Bank is implemented satisfactorily. Other official bilateral and commercial creditors would be expected to offer at least comparable terms for the flow rescheduling and for the stock-of-debt operation. Donors, official bilateral creditors,

FIGURE 1. SUMMARY OF ENHANCED HIPC INITIATIVE ELIGIBILITY REQUIREMENT: IDA-ONLY AND ESAF (PRGF)-ELIGIBLE

First Stage

- *Paris Club* provides flow rescheduling on Naples terms, that is, rescheduling of debt service on eligible debt falling due in the three-year consolidation period (up to 67 percent reduction on eligible maturities on a net present value basis).
- *Other* bilateral and commercial creditors provide at least comparable treatment.
- *Multilateral institutions* continue to provide concessional financing in the framework of World Bank and IMF-supported adjustment programs.
- *Country* establishes first three-year track record of good performance, including, to the extent possible, adoption and implementation of an agreed comprehensive framework for poverty reduction.

Decision Point

Either → **Exit**

- Paris Club stock-of-debt operation under Naples terms (up to 67 percent present value reduction of eligible debt) and comparable treatment by other bilateral and commercial creditors is adequate for the country to reach sustainability measured at the decision point—country not eligible for HIPC Initiative assistance. Sustainability targets: 150 percent NPV of debt-to-export ratio; or 250 percent NPV of debt-to-fiscal revenue ratio for country reaching qualifying thresholds (30 percent export-to-GDP ratio and 15 percent revenue-to-GDP ratio).

Or → **Qualifiers for Assistance**

- Hypothetical Paris Club stock-of-debt operation (on Naples terms) not sufficient for the country's overall debt to become sustainable at the decision point. Country requests additional support under the HIPC Initiative, and IMF and World Bank Boards determine eligibility. International community commits sufficient assistance to reach the sustainability target of NPV of debt-to-export ratio of 150 percent, plus any additional assistance required to meet the NPV of debt-to-revenue target of 250 percent if the country meets the qualifying thresholds. This relief is delivered over the second stage, and the remainder at the completion point, when the country has implemented the pre-agreed key structural and social reforms provided the macroeconomic program remains on track.

Second Stage

- *Paris Club* goes beyond Naples terms to provide more concessional debt reduction in present value terms.
- *Other* bilateral and commercial creditors provide at least comparable treatment.
- *Multilateral institutions* provide enhanced support through interim measures, including relief on debt service falling due.
- *Donors* also provide interim assistance.
- *Country* establishes a second track record of strong performance under Bank/IMF-supported programs, including the implementation of an agreed comprehensive framework of poverty reduction.
- *Country* also takes steps to strengthen debt management.
- Length of second stage is determined by the speed by which country implements pre-agreed key structural reforms designed to achieve sustainable development and poverty reduction.

Floating Completion Point

- Is reached when country implements a comprehensive poverty reduction strategy involving agreed key structural and social reforms and macroeconomic framework designed to promote growth. All creditors provide equal reduction (in NPV terms) on their claims after the application of Naples terms sufficient with interim relief to reach sustainability target. This debt relief is provided with no further policy conditionality.

and multilateral institutions provide financial assistance in the form of grants and concessional loans; the World Bank provides IDA grants and supplemental IDA allocations during this period. At the completion point, the stock-of-debt operation on Lyon terms committed to by Paris Club creditors at the time of the decision point takes effect, and multilateral institutions provide the committed reduction in the NPV of their claims proportional to that provided by bilateral creditors as a group. The IMF provides assistance to a country at the completion point through a special ESAF grant[5] paid into an escrow account and used to cover debt service to the IMF. The World Bank provides assistance at the completion point through the HIPC Trust Fund.

The six-year performance period under the Initiative has been implemented flexibly on a case-by-case basis, with countries receiving credit for already established track records (including for programs supported by IMF emergency assistance for postconflict situations)[6] leading up to the decision point. The period of three years between the decision and the completion point has been shortened for six of the seven countries that have so far reached decision points and been judged eligible for assistance.

Progress in Implementation

From the inception of the HIPC Initiative until September 1999, the Executive Boards of the World Bank and IMF considered 14 countries for eligibility under the HIPC Initiative and agreed to extend assistance to seven (in chronological order): Uganda, Bolivia, Burkina Faso, Guyana, Côte d'Ivoire, Mozambique, and Mali (see Table 1). Assuming continuing good policy performance, debt relief expected for all seven countries under the initial framework of the HIPC Initiative totals more than \$6 billion in nominal terms and will reduce the NPV of all these countries' debt by over \$3 billion, or an average of one-fifth.

In April 1998, *Uganda* became the first country to reach its completion point under the HIPC Initiative. Uganda is receiving assistance equivalent to approximately \$650 million in nominal terms, or 20 percent of its outstanding debt; this reduced Uganda's NPV of debt-to-export ratio to less

[5]In countries facing a hump of debt service, a loan could be provided; in practice, all assistance to date has been in the form of grants, which is expected to continue.

[6]As agreed in September 1998.

TABLE 1. RELIEF UNDER THE ORIGINAL HIPC INITIATIVE

Country	Decision point	Completion point	Total debt relief, nominal (millions of U.S. dollars)	Assistance (in present value terms at the completion point)		
				Percent reduction in debt	All creditors (millions of U.S. dollars)	IMF (millions of U.S. dollars)
Uganda	Apr. 1997	Apr. 1998	650	20	347	69
Bolivia	Sept. 1997	Sept. 1998	760	13	448	29
Burkina Faso	Sept. 1997	Apr. 2000	200	14	115	10
Guyana	Dec. 1997	early 1999	410	24	256	35
Côte d'Ivoire	Mar. 1998	Mar. 2001	800	6	345	23
Mozambique	Apr. 1998	June 1999	3,700	63	1,716	125
Mali	Sept. 1998	Dec. 1999	250	10	128	14
Total			**6,770**	**20**	**3,355**	**305**

than 200 percent. The IMF has provided funds covering about $80 million of debt service over the next nine years.[7]

In September 1998, *Bolivia* reached its completion point under the HIPC Initiative. Total nominal debt relief is about $760 million. The NPV of debt-to-export ratio is reduced to 218 percent and the debt-service ratio will be reduced to about 19 percent in 1999 from 26 percent in 1997. Additional action by a significant bilateral creditor on official development assistance (ODA) claims has reduced the outcome on the NPV of debt-to-export ratio to about 200 percent. In view of Bolivia's relatively high debt-service ratio, delivery of this assistance will be front-loaded, with 40 percent provided by 2002. The IMF's assistance of $30 million in debt-service relief will cover 20 percent of Bolivia's annual debt service to the IMF during 1998–2002.

In May 1999, *Guyana* reached its completion point under the HIPC Initiative and began to receive assistance amounting to $410 million in nominal terms. Of this amount, about $40 million is provided by the IMF, which will cover on average about 26 percent of Guyana's annual debt service to the IMF over the next nine years. In NPV terms, Guyana's creditors will provide debt relief of about $256 million, reducing the NPV of debt-to-export ratio to 115 percent. Guyana was deemed eligible for assistance under the Initiative's fiscal window.

Mozambique reached its completion point in June 1999. The IMF and IDA agreed to increase the assistance beyond the $2.9 billion originally committed in April 1998 to ensure that Mozambique reached the agreed debt sustainability target of an NPV of debt-to-export ratio of 200 percent. The total debt-relief package is about $3.7 billion, or $1.7 billion in NPV terms, of which $145 million will be provided by the IMF to cover part of the debt service falling due to the IMF. This is the largest debt-relief operation by the international financial community under the HIPC Initiative so far, and it reduced Mozambique's debt by almost two-thirds. The debt reduction package was achieved through exceptional efforts by Paris Club creditors in providing assistance on NPV of debt reduction on eligible debt of 90 percent and the provision by Russia—Mozambique's largest

[7]Recent updating of the debt sustainability analysis indicates that since the completion point the NPV of debt-to-export ratio for Uganda is estimated to have risen to 240 percent at the end of 1999 and, in the absence of enhanced HIPC assistance, is estimated to remain above 200 percent over the next three years, partly reflecting lower export earnings from a decline in coffee prices.

creditor—of special treatment on post-cutoff date debt, by bilateral donors in providing voluntary contributions, and the World Bank and IMF in providing more than their proportional share of assistance.

In addition, three countries have reached their decision points and have received commitments of assistance under the HIPC Initiative: *Burkina Faso*, *Côte d'Ivoire*, and *Mali*. Assuming continued good performance in programs supported by the IMF and World Bank, and assurances that other creditors will provide their share of debt relief, Mali could reach its completion point in 1999, Burkina Faso in 2000, and Côte d'Ivoire in 2001. Côte d'Ivoire was deemed eligible for assistance under the Initiative's fiscal window.

Benin and *Senegal* reached their decision points in July 1997 and April 1998, respectively, and were assessed to face sustainable debt burdens after traditional debt-relief mechanisms and, therefore, were deemed not to require assistance under the initial framework of the HIPC Initiative. Their eligibility—along with all the other countries described above—will be reassessed under the enhanced HIPC Initiative.

Preliminary discussions have been held for Guinea-Bissau, Ethiopia, Mauritania, Nicaragua, and Tanzania. By the end of 2000, the eligibility of additional countries—including possibly Cameroon, Chad, Ghana, Guinea, Honduras, Malawi, Niger, Republic of the Congo, Rwanda, Sierra Leone, Togo, Vietnam, Yemen, and Zambia—is expected to be reviewed under the HIPC Initiative. Not all are expected to require assistance.

Modifications to the HIPC Initiative

The creation and initial implementation of the HIPC Initiative has raised widespread interest in the issue of debt relief and prompted suggestions for strengthening the Initiative among religious groups, nongovernmental organizations, the media, international organizations, and governments.[8] In response, the World Bank and IMF jointly launched a comprehensive review of the HIPC Initiative in early 1999 through a public consultative process.

Review of the HIPC Initiative

The consultations were undertaken in two stages. In addition to requesting general views on the HIPC Initiative, the first stage addressed possible modifications to the framework of the Initiative. Responses were solicited from the public on a range of issues relating to the design of the Initiative, including eligibility criteria, the definition of debt sustainability, track record requirements and the timing of debt relief, and links to macroeconomic and structural policy reforms. In addition, views were sought on how to ensure that the mix of resources provided—including balance of payments and budgetary support plus debt relief—best promotes broad-based growth and development. Suggestions were also sought for the financing of any additional cost arising from changes in the HIPC Initiative framework. The second stage focused on strengthening the link between debt relief and poverty reduction. Views were also solicited on how the debt relief provided could be most effectively used to foster social development, and whether more weight should be given to reducing debt-service burdens in the short term rather than the debt overhang. Also sought were suggestions for improving debt management within HIPCs.

[8]The HIPC Initiative and ongoing consultations in this context with civil society have been catalytic in facilitating a broader debate on development and poverty reduction with the World Bank and the IMF. These discussions revealed a strong desire to discuss broader issues of development, aid flows, and poverty reduction, and frequently raised concerns about the current state of development assistance.

The review process brought out three clear messages: a general acknowledgement by most commentators that the HIPC Initiative is a positive step toward a solution to unsustainable debt in that it provides a comprehensive framework for debt relief from all creditors and aims to reduce debts to a sustainable level; widespread calls for speedier implementation of the Initiative; and a desire for a more direct linking of debt relief to poverty reduction measures.

In particular, these suggestions included proposals to:

- *deepen debt relief* through lower target ranges for the NPV of debt-to-export ratio, fuller treatment of the fiscal dimensions of the external debt problem through lower target ranges and thresholds for the fiscal/openness window, greater emphasis on reducing the debt-service burden and lowering post-HIPC Initiative debt service so that governments can adequately meet priority development spending;
- *broaden debt relief* to cover more countries by lowering targets and shortening the performance period;
- *accelerate the delivery of debt relief* by shortening the performance period requirement, placing greater weight on past performance and, related to the Jubilee 2000, to heed the call for the forgiveness of debts before the new millennium;
- *foster greater ownership by debtor governments* of policy targets and a more participatory and transparent process in designing development strategies, increasing the poverty focus of economic and social programs, and ensuring that the savings from debt relief are used exclusively for poverty alleviation; and
- *strengthen transparency and accountability* in debt management by making information about new borrowing arrangements and debt restructurings public, conducting periodic audits into the proper use of borrowed funds, and encouraging a greater involvement of civil society in the HIPC Initiative process.

As a result of the review and consultation exercise, and in line with the proposals endorsed by the June 1999 Group of Seven summit in Cologne, the Boards of the World Bank and IMF in August and September 1999 considered a number of specific modifications for enhancing the Initiative and strengthening the links between debt relief, poverty reduction, and social policies.[9] These modifications were endorsed by the Interim and Development Committees at the fall 1999 IMF-World Bank Annual Meetings.

Modifications to the HIPC Initiative

The enhanced framework of the Initiative incorporates a lowering of targets and thresholds, modified performance requirements, and a strengthening of the link between debt relief and poverty reduction (see Box 1). The modifications also considerably simplify the design and implementation of the Initiative and reduce uncertainties over the amount of debt relief for HIPCs. At the same time, the enhanced Initiative builds on the basic elements that have guided the HIPC Initiative since its inception—notably, the full and equitable participation by all creditors and a focus on sustainable development. These modifications—in particular the strengthening of the Initiative's contribution to the goal of poverty reduction—are closely related to the reform of the ESAF, the IMF's main vehicle for providing support to its low-income member countries. In September 1999, the Interim Committee approved the replacement of the ESAF by a new Poverty Reduction and Growth Facility (PRGF) aimed at making poverty reduction efforts a key and more explicit element of a growth oriented economic strategy.[10]

The main modifications to the HIPC Initiative may be summarized as follows:

Deeper debt relief by:

- lowering the NPV of debt-to-export target to 150 percent from 200–250 percent, thereby replacing the current target range with a single target. A country-specific vulnerability analysis would no longer be required;

[9]Both these papers, prepared jointly by IMF and World Bank staff, as well as the summary of the proposals for changing the HIPC Initiative discussed by the Executive Boards of the Bank and IMF in April, are posted on the websites (http://www.imf.org) of the Bank and IMF. See *Modifications to the Heavily Indebted Poor Countries (HIPC) Initiative,* July 23, 1999, and Public Information Notice (PIN) No. 99/76, and *HIPC Initiative: Strengthening the Links Between Debt Relief and Poverty Reduction*, August 26, 1999.

[10]See *Overview: Transforming the Enhanced Structural Adjustment Facility (ESAF) and the Debt Initiative of Heavily Indebted Poor Countries (HIPCs)* on the IMF's website (http://www.imf.org).

Box 1. Implementation of the HIPC Initiative: Major Changes

Simplification

- Calculation of assistance at decision point on actual data, not projections, for the completion point.
- Apply single NPV of debt-to-export target to all countries rather than decide target on a country-specific basis within target range.
- Elimination of borderline option.

Modifications

- Lower NPV of debt-to-export (150 percent) and debt-to-revenue target (250 percent), with lower thresholds for latter (30 percent export-to-GDP, and 15 percent revenue-to-GDP).
- Floating completion points, with the timing of completion points tied to implementation of key structural reforms and the poverty reduction strategy.
- Earlier delivery of assistance both from decision and completion points.

Principal Changes

Elimination of:

- Projections of position at completion point as basis for assistance;
- Vulnerability analysis as a basis for country-specific determining targets; and
- Target ranges for the completion point.

This will permit a much simplified preliminary HIPC Initiative document that could focus on the track record and proposed timing of the decision point, key structural policies, and enhanced framework for poverty reduction.

Forward-Looking Focus in Decision Point Document Switched to:

- Identification of key structural policies to which floating completion points would be tied;
- Enhanced framework for poverty reduction;
- Country-by-country assessment of appropriate levels for interim relief and front-loading of the delivery of assistance in the light of absorption capacity and projections of key debt indicators; and
- Steps to improve debt management.

At completion point: discretionary reassessment for debt situation with the option of providing more assistance if, as a result of external factors, there has been a major upward deviation in debt outcomes. This would be decided on a case-by-case basis, consulting all creditors involved.

- lowering the NPV of debt-to-fiscal-revenue target to 250 percent from 280 percent and a lowering of the eligibility thresholds for the openness of an economy (export-to-GDP ratio) from 40 to 30 percent and for the revenue effort (revenue-to-GDP ratio) from 20 to 15 percent; and
- changing the assessment base for debt relief under the Initiative, with calculation of debt relief now based on actual data for the year prior to the decision point rather than on projections for the completion point. In most cases, this change in the calculation is likely to result in higher assistance since the debt ratios targeted under the Initiative have typically declined as economic reforms take hold. In addition, as a result of this change, there will no longer be a need for automatic reassessment at the completion point of the amount of assistance to be provided.

Faster debt relief through:

- providing interim relief by international financial institutions between the decision and completion points;
- front-loading the delivery of the remaining debt relief provided by international financial institutions after the completion point. The acceleration of assistance through front-loaded and interim relief should not, however, exceed the country's absorptive capacity and the resulting time profile of debt relief should not jeopardize the achievement of debt sustainability over the medium term; and
- introducing floating completion points under which the assessment of a country's performance in the second stage is based on specific outcomes on policy reform and the maintenance of macroeconomic stability, rather than the length of the track record. The use of floating completion points provides an incentive to implement reforms quickly, thereby permitting strong performers to reach the completion point earlier. It also allows HIPCs greater ownership over the reform timetable.

Broader debt relief through:

- a greater safety margin for the achievement of debt sustainability, providing a clear and permanent exit from unsustainable indebtedness at the completion point. This will increase the number of countries that could potentially qualify for HIPC Initiative assistance to 36 from 29, and possibly more (see Box 2).[11]

Strengthened Links Between Debt Relief and Poverty Reduction

From the outset, progress in social sector policies and in poverty reduction has been an integral part of the design of the HIPC Initiative. Indeed, as with conditions on macroeconomic and structural reforms, countries must meet performance requirements in the social sectors to receive HIPC Initiative assistance. In the early cases in which countries reached their completion points, they made significant progress in implementing social reforms, aided by higher budgetary allocations for social spending. More generally, in most HIPCs, budgetary spending on health and education has been larger than actual debt-service payments, and HIPCs have typically received twice as much by way of aid flows than they have paid in debt service (see Box 3). Progress in addressing poverty in the early cases under the Initiative, however, has been uneven. For example, not all countries have developed comprehensive poverty reduction strategies and, where these are in place, they have typically not incorporated specific targeted improvements in key social indicators.

Building on the progress to date, the enhanced framework for poverty reduction is based on the premise that the best way to ensure a robust link between debt relief and poverty reduction is to make HIPC Initiative debt relief an integral part of broader efforts to implement outcome-oriented poverty reduction strategies using all available resources. This requires a nationally owned, comprehensive poverty reduction strategy which recognizes that:

- sustained poverty reduction requires rapid economic growth, and that macroeconomic stability and structural reforms are essential for moving to a higher path of sustained growth;

[11]Eligibility under the enhanced HIPC Initiative will be assessed on a case-by-case basis and is not limited to the countries included in the group of 41 HIPCs that was established early on for analytical purposes. Rather, if a country meets the criteria of the enhanced Initiative, it could be eligible for assistance: that is, a country that is IDA-only and ESAF (PRGF)-eligible, has established a minimum three-year track record of satisfactory performance under World Bank- and IMF-supported programs, and at the decision point has debt ratios—after the full use of traditional debt-relief mechanisms—above the sustainability targets. Countries that have not yet adopted those programs would need to do so by the end of 2000, the deadline (sunset clause) for meeting the entry requirement.

Box 2. Countries Expected to Qualify for HIPC Initiative Assistance

Decision points expected for 1999 and 2000	*Decision points expected for 2001 or later*
Benin[1]	Burundi
Bolivia[2]	Central African Republic[5]
Burkina Faso[3]	Congo, Dem. Rep.
Cameroon	Liberia
Chad	Myanmar
Congo, Rep.	São Tomé and Príncipe
Côte d'Ivoire[3]	Somalia
Ethiopia	Sudan
Ghana[4]	
Guyana[2]	
Honduras[5]	
Lao People's Dem. Rep.[5]	
Madagascar	
Malawi	
Mali[3]	
Mauritania	
Mozambique[2]	
Nicaragua	
Niger	
Rwanda	
Senegal[1]	
Sierra Leone	
Tanzania	
Togo[5]	
Uganda[2]	
Zambia	

[1]Countries not requiring assistance under original HIPC Initiative but now eligible for reconsideration for assistance under the enhanced HIPC Initiative.

[2]Countries that have already received assistance under the original HIPC Initiative (i.e., have reached the completion point).

[3]Countries to which assistance had been committed under original HIPC Initiative (i.e., had reached the decision point).

[4]The country has indicated that it does not want to be considered for assistance under the enhanced HIPC Initiative.

[5]Countries that would benefit from assistance under the enhanced HIPC Initiative but that were considered unlikely to benefit from the original HIPC Initiative.

- poverty is multidimensional, and poverty reduction requires more than the delivery of improved social services;
- broad-based participation of civil society and strengthened governance is essential to the sustained implementation of an anti-poverty strategy; and

Box 3. HIPCs: Debt Service Due Versus Paid, Social Spending, and External Inflows

What is the likely magnitude of the reduction in annual debt-service payments that could result from the implementation of the enhanced HIPC Initiative? Any estimates of the nominal decline in debt-service payments are inevitably tentative. Nonetheless, they illustrate the significance of the possible cash-flow impact of debt relief in relation to current levels of GDP, exports, gross inflows of foreign aid, and social spending for a sample of HIPCs.

Before turning to this issue, recent data on HIPCs' debt-service payments should be placed in a similar context. Some commentators have argued that debt-service payments by HIPCs have often exceeded social spending by a substantial margin. However, it is important to base these comparisons on *actual* debt service payments—this is, after debt relief—rather than scheduled debt service, which is the concept used in balance of payments methodology. Most HIPCs have benefited from a significant reduction in the debt service burden before assistance under the HIPC Initiative, but this debt relief is not reflected in a corresponding decline in scheduled debt service as recorded in the balance of payments. For example, in 1998 scheduled debt service on Mozambique's public external debt amounted to $396 million, whereas debt service actually paid in 1998 was $109 million, or slightly more than one-quarter of the scheduled amount.[1] By comparison, Mozambique's expenditure on health and education in 1998—excluding some spending financed by external aid flows—amounted to about $120 million.

Comparing debt service paid and social spending alone also provides only a partial view of the relationship between international official resource flows and social spending. Again, Mozambique illustrates the point: in 1998, gross external financing (in new loans and grants) amounted to almost $713 million. Thus, after debt-service payments, the net official resources flow to Mozambique in 1998 was nearly $604 million, or more than four times the recorded total of education and health spending.

A similar picture is evident for many other HIPCs. The Figure illustrates for the first seven cases, as well as all 28 HIPCs where data are available, the relationship between debt service paid in 1993–97, gross external financing, and social spending. Gross external financing inflows significantly exceed social spending and debt service paid for the seven HIPCs that have reached their decision point. Gross inflows of external assistance averaged some 14

[1]A rescheduling of payments falling due actually increases the scheduled debt service recorded in the balance of payments, as a result of the additional payments due resulting from the rescheduling. A counterbalancing item of debt relief obtained is shown in the financing section of the balance of payments. The difference between these two items is the cash debt service expected to be paid.

percent of GDP for this group, while their expenditures on health and education averaged about 6 percent of GDP, and debt service paid, about 7 percent. Aggregate data reveal a similar picture for the broader group of 28 HIPCs for which data are available. While average service paid was some 6 percent of GDP for this group and social spending averaged 5 percent of GDP, for most of these countries social spending actually exceeded debt service paid.

Implementation of the enhanced HIPC Initiative framework for the seven countries that have reached decision points would result in lower debt service payments, on average by about one-third, or some 2 percent of GDP, in the five years after the completion point, compared with the five years to 1997. While these calculations are only illustrative and differ in individual HIPCs, they indicate relative magnitudes. At these levels, the savings from debt relief could represent a significant contribution to social spending in HIPCs even though other official development flows are likely to remain the major source of external resources available for this purpose (see Figure).

EXTERNAL DEBT SERVICE PAID, GROSS EXTERNAL FINANCING, AND SOCIAL SPENDING

(In percent of GDP, average for 1993–97)

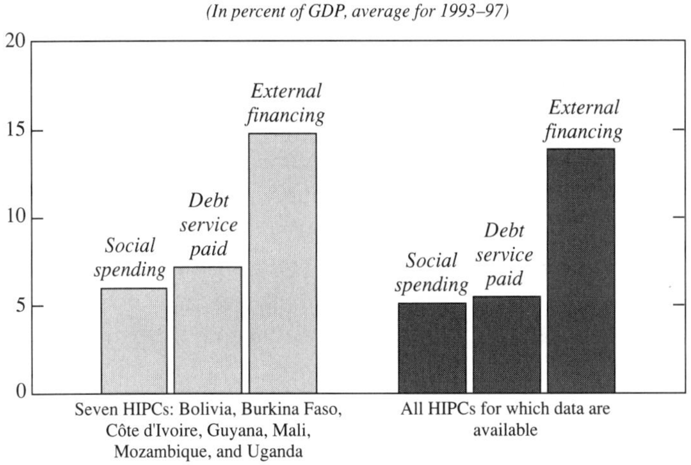

Source: IMF estimates.

Note: Comprehensive data on social spending are not available for all HIPCs, but only for 28 countries. Social spending is defined as health and education spending. Excludes countries where only one category of spending is available, and those where only partial expenditure (current or capital) are available.

- focusing on transparent outcome-oriented goals (in the context of the International Development Goals for 2015,[12] such as the objective of halving poverty) and establishing mechanisms for the broad-based monitoring of related indicators is essential for the design and implementation of a poverty reduction strategy.

The nationally owned poverty reduction strategy would be reflected in a new vehicle—a *Poverty Reduction Strategy Paper (PRSP)*—which, to the extent possible, should be in place when a country reaches its decision point under the HIPC Initiative. However, on a transitional basis, the decision point could be agreed while a poverty reduction strategy is being formulated. In all cases, progress in implementing the poverty reduction strategy would be required by the completion point. Although the PRSP would initially be introduced in countries qualifying for HIPC Initiative assistance, it would eventually be extended to all countries eligible for the Poverty Reduction and Growth Facility and resources from the World Bank's IDA and serve as the basis for all Bank and IMF lending to low-income countries.

The PRSP would:

- outline the poverty reduction strategy and be produced by the authorities in close collaboration with the World Bank, IMF, and other multilateral institutions and donors, in a way that ensures transparency and broad-based participation in the choice of goals, the formulation of policies, and the monitoring of implementation, with ownership by the government;
- ensure consistency between a country's macroeconomic, structural, and social policies (including their sequencing) and the goals of poverty reduction and social development, including establishing priorities in these areas. It would also indicate the country-specific resource needs to achieve the 2015 International Development Goals;
- address the obstacles to rapid growth and diffusion of the benefits of participation in this growth to the poor and propose actions to deal with these obstacles; and
- be endorsed by the Executive Boards of the World Bank and the IMF as the framework for each institution's lending operations, and

[12]See Glossary of Terms for a fuller description of these goals.

be published. It should also serve as a basis for support by donors, regional development banks, and other multilateral institutions.

These enhancements to the HIPC Initiative are part of a coherent strategy to help poor countries move on to a sustainable faster growth path and to have the IMF and World Bank focus on poverty reduction as a fundamental goal of their operations in these countries. In line with this, the key element in the transformation of the IMF's ESAF into the Poverty Reduction and Growth Facility is to base future lending to low-income member countries on the comprehensive, nationally owned, and outcome-oriented poverty reduction strategy elaborated in the country's PRSP. The complementarity of macroeconomic, structural, and social policies will now be given greater recognition, and the PRSP will provide a new vehicle to integrate these policies—including their costs—in a mutually reinforcing manner. Furthermore, greater emphasis will be placed on good governance—especially full transparency and effective monitoring of government budgets and the efficiency of social expenditures. PRSPs will also provide a new framework for closer collaboration between the World Bank and the IMF.

Costs and Financing

The total cost of the enhanced HIPC framework is estimated at $27.4 billion in 1998 NPV terms ($50 billion in nominal terms) for 33 HIPCs expected to qualify (excluding Liberia, Somalia, and Sudan),[13] or more than double the total cost of $12.5 billion estimated for the previous framework. Given the magnitudes involved, decisions on the enhancements to the Initiative have proceeded in parallel with agreement on additional financing for the IMF's contribution to the HIPC Initiative, as well as that of other multilateral creditors, and the World Bank in particular. Under the enhanced framework, the shares of HIPC Initiative costs for bilateral and multilateral creditors are estimated to remain roughly equal. Overall costs to multilateral creditors are projected to rise to $13.3 billion under the enhanced framework (excluding Liberia, Somalia, and Sudan) from $6.2 billion under the original framework.

[13]Policy slippages as well as armed conflict or domestic unrest in some countries could delay these countries' decision points. Total costs in 1998 NPV terms including Liberia, Somalia, and Sudan are estimated at approximately $19 billion under the original framework and $36 billion under the enhanced framework.

Paris Club bilateral creditors have agreed to increase debt reduction in NPV terms to up to 90 percent or more, if needed, on commercial loans, on a case-by-case basis, as well as provide additional relief on ODA claims—up to full cancellation—on a bilateral basis.

Non-Paris Club official creditors and commercial creditors would be expected to provide debt relief on terms comparable with those of the Paris Club. A number of HIPCs have encountered difficulties in obtaining such comparable relief from bilateral creditors not participating in the Paris Club. Particular concern has been expressed by some developing countries about the impact on their economies of providing terms comparable to the Paris Club on their claims on HIPCs. Efforts by all sides will need to be intensified in order to attain more satisfactory outcomes where all creditors contribute their share in making the enhanced Initiative a success in providing HIPCs with a durable exit from their external debt problems.

Some regional *multilateral creditors* are likely to face difficulties in financing enhancements to the HIPC Initiative from their own resources and would need to rely on bilateral contributions to cover their full share of the expected additional debt relief. The IMF's contribution to the enhanced HIPC Initiative is expected to rise to $2.3 billion from $1.2 billion under the original framework. This is to be financed by additional bilateral contributions and off-market gold sales. The World Bank's share of financing is expected to increase to $5.1 billion from $2.4 billion under the original framework, and is to be financed through bilateral contributions to the HIPC Trust Fund and from the Bank's own resources. Funding efforts to help cover the Bank's costs and those of other multilateral institutions are continuing.

Preliminary IMF staff estimates indicate that at the end of 1997, the debt stock, in present value terms, of countries likely to receive assistance under the Initiative was about $100 billion (or some $137 billion in nominal terms); after full application of traditional debt-relief mechanisms, this would be reduced to about $72 billion in present value terms. Implementation of the enhanced HIPC Initiative would further reduce this stock of debt by almost $27 billion. In short, external debt of these countries would decline by about 60 percent of its end-1997 value as a result of full application of traditional debt-relief mechanisms and the enhanced HIPC Initiative.[14]

[14]See Daseking and Powell, "From Toronto Terms to the HIPC Initiative: A Brief History of Debt Relief to Low-Income Countries," IMF Working Paper No. 99/142, October 1999. This paper also estimates that traditional debt relief mechanisms (that is, before HIPC Ini-

Implementation

The enhanced HIPC Initiative will be implemented in accordance with the principles that have guided the Initiative since its inception, notably that debt relief be additional and its financing should not compromise other resource transfers to poor countries; that the financial integrity of multilateral financial institutions be maintained; and that cost sharing be on a broad and equitable basis. It builds on existing mechanisms for providing debt relief from the Paris Club and other official bilateral and commercial creditors, as well as from multilateral creditors.

Assistance resulting from the modifications to the HIPC Initiative is to be available to all qualifying countries, including those that have already reached their decision and completion points under the original framework of the Initiative. The approach to providing retroactive treatment detailed below ensures that countries are not penalized for early qualification for HIPC Initiative assistance, allows revised debt targets established under the Initiative to apply at the time that enhanced assistance is provided, and ensures that the country's policy performance remains satisfactory at the time any additional assistance is provided. In particular, the timing of the proposed additional debt relief should be determined, among other things, on an assessment of progress in designing and implementing a comprehensive poverty reduction strategy.

- Existing commitments made on the basis of the original framework (for example, for Mali, Burkina Faso, and Côte d'Ivoire) would, with continued strong policy implementation, be delivered at the existing completion points.
- Evaluation of enhanced debt relief would be based on countries' current situations so as to ensure that the country will be at, or below, the newly established debt sustainability thresholds. This would require an updated debt sustainability analysis, based on the latest available macroeconomic and external debt data, as well as discount rates, as the basis for calculating the required topping-up of HIPC Initiative assistance.

---

tiative assistance) provided relief to HIPCs in present value terms of at least $30 billion from Paris Club creditors, including the Russian Federation, and non-Paris Club official bilateral and commercial creditors.

- Proposals for enhanced assistance would be submitted to the Executive Boards of the World Bank and IMF for approval in principle. Board approval would allow the staffs to seek agreement to enhanced assistance from the Paris Club and other multilateral creditors consistent with proportional burden sharing. Once the participation of all creditors in the enhanced HIPC assistance was confirmed, and their financing assured, the additional assistance would be committed by the Bank and IMF Boards, and could be delivered in part during the interim period, namely the period between the decision and the completion points.

Supporting Policies

As stated earlier, the HIPC Initiative is not a panacea for the economic and poverty problems of the HIPCs. Even if, hypothetically, all of the external debt of the HIPCs was forgiven, most of these countries would still depend on significant levels of concessional external assistance for many years. As implied by the time horizon of the International Development Goals for 2015, significant poverty reduction can only be achieved through sustained economic growth, which will require efforts over many years. The effectiveness of the enhanced HIPC Initiative depends on its success in fostering the continued implementation of the policies required to achieve poverty reduction and sustainable development. This includes sustaining sound macroeconomic policies and structural reforms—including forcefully addressing problems of governance, accelerating public sector reform, and further liberalizing trade, exchange, and financial systems. These policies must be supported by higher aid flows—from the current historically low levels—that are well targeted. Both the experience of the donor community and research on aid effectiveness show that aid can have a significant effect on growth and poverty reduction when it is accompanied by a strong policy environment and a sustained adjustment effort. Indeed, there is scope for a better allocation of aid resources to countries with severe poverty but good policies.[15]

[15]See Burnside and Dollar, "Aid, Policies and Growth," Policy Research Working Paper No. 1777, World Bank, 1997, and Collier and Dollar, "Aid Allocation and Poverty Reduction," Policy Research Working Paper No. 2041, World Bank, 1999.

Unfettered and guaranteed access for all exports from low-income countries to industrial country markets is also crucial for higher growth and the integration of HIPCs into the world economy. Finally, prudent debt management in the HIPCs, reinforced by restraints by industrial countries on nonconcessional lending—including eschewing any lending for nonproductive purposes, including through the use of officially guaranteed export credits—remains central to ensuring a durable exit from an unsustainable debt burden.

The adoption of the nationally owned Poverty Reduction Strategy Paper represents a new paradigm for integrating poverty reduction efforts through coherent macroeconomic policies, structural reforms, and social policies consistent with this overarching goal. The international community must now move rapidly to support the country-specific implementation of PRSPs. This poses a major, and critically important, challenge to all parties involved in efforts to improve the quality of life of the poor of the world as we approach the new millennium.

Glossary of Terms

The following terms are used throughout the pamphlet. For a more detailed glossary, see IMF, Official Financing for Developing Countries, *World Economic and Financial Surveys, February 1998 (Appendix II).*

Bilateral creditors. These are government creditors, whose claims are loans extended, or guaranteed, by governments or official agencies, such as export credit agencies. Certain official creditors participate in debt reschedulings under the aegis of the Paris Club (see below).

Brady Plan. An approach adopted in the late 1980s to restructure debt of developing countries to commercial banks, which emphasizes voluntary market-based debt- and debt-service-reduction (DDSR) operations. The cornerstone of DDSR operations is some combination of a buyback at a discount and the issuance of "Brady bonds" by the debtor country in exchange for banks' claims. Such operations complement countries' efforts to restore external viability through the adoption of medium-term structural adjustment programs supported by the IMF and other multilateral and official bilateral creditors.

Cologne terms. Concessional debt reduction agreed by the Paris Club in 1999 as part of the enhanced Initiative for Heavily Indebted Poor Countries. Under these terms, Paris Club creditors agree on a case-by-case basis on a net present value debt reduction of up to 90 percent on pre-cutoff date commercial (non-ODA) debt, or more if this is required in the context of equal burden sharing (after traditional debt-relief mechanisms) with multilateral creditors to achieve debt sustainability in a particular country case.

Completion point. A point at which the country concerned receives the bulk of its assistance under the HIPC Initiative, without any further policy conditions. The timing of the completion point depends:

- under the initial framework of the HIPC Initiative, on the completion of a second track record period of good performance under adjustment programs supported by the IMF and the World Bank; or
- under the enhanced Initiative, on the country's implementation of pre-agreed key structural reforms including the PRSP (floating completion point).

Debt service-to-export ratio. Scheduled debt service (interest and principal payments due on public and publicly guaranteed debt during a year) for the same coverage of debt as in the NPV debt-to-export ratio, expressed as a percent of exports for that year.

Debt sustainability. Under the original HIPC Initiative, debt sustainability targets were decided on a country-specific basis in the range of a 200–250 percent NPV of debt-to-export ratio; for highly open economies (with export-to-GDP ratios of at least 40 percent) and which raised more than 20 percent of GDP by way of revenues, a lower target could be established consistent with a NPV debt-to-revenue ratio of 280 percent. Assistance under the Initiative was calibrated to reach these targets at the completion point. Under the enhanced HIPC Initiative, a single NPV of debt-to-export target of 150 percent was agreed (as opposed to the earlier range) and the fiscal target was lowered to 250 percent of NPV of debt-to-revenue ratio, with the eligibility thresholds reduced to 30 percent for the export-to-GDP ratio and 15 percent for the revenue-to-GDP ratio. In addition, these targets were to be calculated at the decision point (rather than the completion point as was the case under the original framework of the Initiative).

Debt sustainability analysis. A study undertaken jointly by staff of the IMF and the World Bank and the country concerned, in consultation with creditors, at the decision point. On the basis of this analysis, the country's eligibility for assistance under the HIPC Initiative is determined.

Decision point. A point at which a HIPC completes its first (three-year) track record of good performance under adjustment programs supported by the IMF and the World Bank, and when, based on the debt sustainability analysis, a country's eligibility for assistance under the HIPC Initiative is determined.

Heavily indebted poor countries (HIPCs). As used initially for analytical purposes: a group of 41 developing countries, including 32 countries with a 1993 GNP per capita of $695 or less and 1993 present value of debt to exports higher than 220 percent or present value of debt to GNP higher than 80 percent. This group also included nine countries that have received concessional rescheduling from Paris Club creditors (or are potentially eligible for such rescheduling). However, this concept evolved in the course of implementing the Initiative to include all countries eligible for the Enhanced Structural Adjustment Facility (ESAF) and eligible only for concessional financing from the World Bank (IDA-only) that face unsustainable debt situations even after traditional debt-relief mechanisms are applied fully. Countries must also undertake adjustment programs supported by the IMF and the World Bank.

HIPC Initiative. Framework adopted jointly by the IMF and the World Bank in 1996 for action to resolve the external debt problems of heavily indebted poor countries. The Initiative envisages comprehensive debt relief by the international financial community—including the multilateral institutions—to achieve debt sustainability, provided a country builds a track record of strong policy performance. The framework was strengthened in 1999 (enhanced HIPC Initiative) to provide faster, deeper, and broader debt relief.

HIPC Trust Fund. The HIPC Trust Fund, established by the World Bank, provides debt relief to eligible HIPCs on debt owed to participating multilaterals. It either prepays, or purchases a portion of the debt owed to a multilateral creditor and cancels such debt, or pays debt service as it comes due. The HIPC Trust Fund is administered by the IDA and receives contributions from participating multilateral creditors and from bilateral donors. Contributions can be earmarked for debt owed by a particular debtor or to a particular multilateral creditor. Donors can also provide contributions to an unallocated pool and would participate in decisions regarding the use of these unallocated funds. The overall structure of the Trust Fund allows multilateral creditors to participate in the Trust Fund in ways consistent with their financial policies. It also addresses the resource constraints for certain multilateral creditors and the potential requirements of donors.

IMF emergency and postconflict assistance. Since 1962, the IMF has provided emergency assistance in the form of outright drawings to help members overcome balance of payments problems arising from sudden and unforeseeable natural disasters. This assistance was extended in September 1995 to cover certain postconflict situations. Assistance for countries in postconflict situations, as well as for natural disasters, is normally limited to 25 percent of quota and is available only if the member intends to move within a relatively short time to an upper credit tranche arrangement with the IMF.

Interim Assistance. Debt relief provided between the decision and completion points. Under the enhanced HIPC Initiative, the Bank and IMF have agreed to join the Paris Club in providing such debt relief.

International Development Association (IDA). IDA is the concessional lending arm of the World Bank Group, providing financing to low-income member countries.

International Development Goals for 2015. As a major step toward concerted international action for development, the OECD and the United Nations have agreed to focus on a series of key goals in partnership with developing countries. These goals have been endorsed by major international conferences. They give an integrated world view of human well-being in its economic, social, and environmental aspects. The set is continuously developed and updated to show results achieved and the efforts to be made to reach these goals up to the year 2015. These goals include, among other things, reduction in the proportion of people living in extreme poverty in developing countries by at least one half by 2015; achievement of universal primary education in all countries by 2015; reduction in death rates for infants and children under the age of five years in each developing country by two thirds the 1990 level by 2015; and reduction in rate of maternal mortality by three fourths between 1990 and 2015.

Jubilee 2000. Jubilee 2000 is an international grass roots movement with a presence in more than 40 countries advocating a debt-free start to the millennium for indebted poor countries.

Lyon terms. Concessional debt reduction agreed by the Paris Club in 1996 as part of the HIPC Initiative. Under these terms, Paris Club creditors can agree on a case-by-case basis to reduce pre-cutoff date commercial (non-ODA) debt up to 80 percent in NPV terms.

Multilateral creditors. These creditors are multilateral institutions such as the IMF and the World Bank, and other regional multilateral development banks, such as the African Development Bank and the Inter-American Development Bank.

Naples terms. Concessional debt-rescheduling terms for low-income countries approved by the Paris Club in December 1994 and applied on a case-by-case basis. Countries can receive a reduction of pre-cutoff date commercial (non-ODA) debt of up to 67 percent in net present value terms. These terms, along with comparable action by other non-multilateral creditors, are known as traditional debt-relief mechanisms.

Net present value (NPV) of debt. The sum of all future debt-service obligations (interest and principal) on existing debt, discounted at the market interest rate. Whenever the interest rate on a loan is lower than the market interest rate, the resulting NPV of debt is smaller than its face value, with the difference reflecting the grant element.

Net present value (NPV) of debt-to-export ratio. Net present value (NPV) of outstanding public and publicly guaranteed external debt at the end of the period, expressed as a percent of exports of goods and services.

Official development assistance (ODA). ODA is defined by the Organization for Economic Cooperation and Development (OECD) as grants or loans extended by a government on concessional terms to developing countries with the promotion of economic development and welfare as the main objective. The minimum grant element is 25 percent based on a fixed discount rate of 10 percent.

Off-market gold sales. In September 1999, the IMF's Executive Board agreed in principle to conduct a one-time, off-market transaction of up to 14 million fine ounces of gold. On the basis of market prices, the IMF will sell gold to some central banks of member countries with repayment obligations to the IMF, with the understanding that these central banks will use the gold to make the repayment. These transactions will allow the IMF to place an amount of the sales proceeds equivalent to SDR 35 an ounce in the general resources account, and the balance will be placed in a special account with the interest proceeds benefiting the ESAF-HIPC Trust. The net effect of these transactions will leave the IMF's holdings of physical gold unchanged as no gold will be released to the market. As a result, there will be no impact on the supply and demand balance in the gold market.

Paris Club. Informal group of creditor governments mainly from industrial countries (that is, the OECD) that has met on a regular basis in Paris since 1956 with the French Treasury providing the Secretariat. Creditors meet with debtor countries to agree with them on restructuring their debts as part of the international support provided to a country that is experiencing debt-servicing difficulties and is pursuing an adjustment program supported by an arrangement with the IMF.

Poverty Reduction and Growth Facility (PRGF). This facility agreed in late 1999 will replace the Enhanced Structural Adjustment Facility (ESAF) as the IMF's concessional lending arm; its goal is to make poverty reduction efforts among low-income members a key and more explicit element of a renewed growth-oriented economic strategy. The cornerstones of the new approach, which will continue to be based on sound macroeconomic policies, would include a comprehensive, nationally owned Poverty Reduction Strategy Paper (PRSP), social and sectoral programs aimed at poverty reduction, greater emphasis on good governance, and priority to key reform measures critical to achieving the member government's social goals.

Poverty Reduction Strategy Paper (PRSP). In the context of strengthening the link between debt relief and poverty reduction, in September 1999 the Executive Boards of the IMF and the World Bank agreed to introduce Poverty Reduction Strategy Papers to be prepared by national authorities in close collaboration with World Bank and IMF staff. These papers would be country-driven; developed transparently with broad participation of elected institutions, stakeholders, including civil society, key donors, and regional banks; include monitorable outcome indicators; and have a clear link with the agreed International Development Goals for 2015. PRSPs will provide the basis for all IDA and IMF lending to low-income countries and will gradually replace current Policy Framework Papers.

Structural Adjustment Facility (SAF)/Enhanced Structural Adjustment Facility (ESAF). The SAF, established in 1986 and no longer operational, and the ESAF, established in 1987 and extended and enlarged in 1993, are the concessional loan windows of the IMF. These facilities are available to low-income member countries.

Traditional debt-relief mechanisms. See Naples terms.